Advances in Mental Health and Addiction

SpringerBriefs in Advances in Mental Health and Addiction

Series Editor

Masood Zangeneh, Humber College, Woodbridge, Canada

Over the past several decades we have witnessed dramatic shifts in prevailing approaches to mental health and addiction. Significant scientific achievements have led to novel treatment options that impacted the experiences of individuals with mental disorders. In recent years, new perspectives have begun to influence the way we address mental health and substance dependencies, resulting in a greater emphasis on mental health promotion and prevention strategies. Despite these progressions, mental health care systems too often remain stagnant, fragmented, and peripheral.

This sub-series provides an opportunity to expand upon cutting-edge research being presented at mental health or addiction related conferences or colloquia around the world. Each volume is dedicated to a singular event and provides an opportunity for scholars to present their research and get feedback from other scholars in their field.

Sachin Batra
Editor

Thriving in the Workplace

Inclusivity, Digital Work, and Well-Being

Springer

Editor
Sachin Batra
NICMAR University
Pune, Maharashtra, India

ISSN 2570-3390 ISSN 2570-3404 (electronic)
Advances in Mental Health and Addiction
ISSN 2948-2224 ISSN 2948-2232 (electronic)
SpringerBriefs in Advances in Mental Health and Addiction
ISBN 978-3-032-06157-7 ISBN 978-3-032-06158-4 (eBook)
https://doi.org/10.1007/978-3-032-06158-4

This Springer imprint is published by the registered company Springer Nature Switzerland AG
The registered company address is: Gewerbestrasse 11, 6330 Cham, Switzerland

Preface

The twenty-first-century workplace is undergoing a seismic transformation which is shaped by digital disruption, the rapid integration of artificial intelligence (AI), and evolving expectations of employee health and well-being. While these changes bring promising opportunities for innovation and efficiency, they also pose significant challenges for mental health, social inclusion, and workplace equity. This book, *Thriving in the Workplace*: *Inclusivity, Digital Work and Well-Being*, explores the emerging contours of these challenges and offers multidisciplinary perspectives on how individuals and organizations can navigate them.

The chapters included in this volume reflect a commitment to inclusive inquiry, critical reflection, and evidence-based exploration. They delve into topics often overlooked in mainstream organizational discourse, such as the mental health needs of neurodiverse individuals in vocational settings, the psychological toll of hyperconnectivity and digital overload, and the subtle but damaging effects of social exclusion at work.

In "A Critical Analysis of Mental Well-Being among Vocational Training Students with Intellectual Disabilities having Autism," the authors advocate for more responsive and compassionate training ecosystems that can enable neurodiverse individuals to flourish in the world of work. "Revealing the Unseen Face of Digital Workplaces" unpacks how phenomena like information overload, anxiety, and the fear of missing out (FOMO) can undermine well-being in tech-driven work cultures. The final chapter, "Health and Wellness in Modern Workplace: A Bibliometric Perspective on Ostracism and Well-Being," offers a structured mapping of scholarly trends, signaling growing academic concern about the psychosocial dynamics that influence employee health.

Together, these contributions highlight a critical imperative: technological advancement must be accompanied by human-centered policies and practices. Thriving in the modern workplace is not just about adapting to change; it is about shaping environments where well-being, inclusion, and dignity are foundational.

This book is intended for scholars, HR professionals, policymakers, organizational leaders, and advocates of workplace equity and mental health. As we imagine the future of work which is increasingly mediated by AI, automation, and digital tools, we must ensure that this future remains anchored in the values of empathy, accessibility, and care.

We extend our heartfelt gratitude to the contributors whose work pushes the boundaries of conventional research and practice. It is our hope that this volume contributes meaningfully to conversations on how we can build healthier, more resilient, and inclusive workplaces in the age of AI.

Pune, India
December 2025

Sachin Batra

Contents

A Critical Analysis of Mental Well-Being Among Vocational Training Students with Intellectual Disabilities Having Autism

Neelam Bansal

Abbreviations

ADL	Activity of daily living
ASD	Autism spectrum disorder
ID	Intellectual disability
MHWB	Mental health and well-being
PWDs	Person with disabilities
WEMWBS	Warwick-Edinburgh Mental Well-being Scale

1 Background of the Study

Mental well-being is a crucial aspect of overall health and encompasses emotional, psychological, and social well-being. It affects thinking, feeling, and behavior, as well as handling of stress, related to others. Promoting mental well-being is essential across all stages of life, from childhood to adulthood. The World Health Organization (WHO) defines positive mental health as a state of health and well-being for the proper functioning of both persons with disabilities and the community. Mental health and well-being is a mental state, in which people realize their own potential and develop strategies for coping with stress and anxiety. This is helpful for more productive and fruitful work and also for active participation and contribution to society. Mental health and well-being involves an individual's mental, emotional, and social well-being, influencing their ability to handle stress,

N. Bansal (✉)
Amity Institute of Rehabilitation Sciences, Amity University Uttar Pradesh Lucknow Campus, Lucknow, Uttar Pradesh, India

S. Batra (ed.), *Thriving in the Workplace*, Advances in Mental Health and Addiction, https://doi.org/10.1007/978-3-032-06158-4_1

maintain relationships, and perform effectively. Students with intellectual disability having autism often face unique challenges, including family, daily life and academic expectations, disability biases, and societal pressures. These challenges can significantly impact their mental health, leading to anxiety and depression. Persons with disabilities (PWDs) are able to experience mental health challenges due to a variety of social, emotional, and physical activities. They may face different challenges such as discrimination, isolation, lack of accessibility, and limited opportunities, which may lead to feelings of anxiety, stress, and depression. For some situations, the disability itself may also be associated with cognitive or emotional difficulties. It is essential to recognize that PWDs, like everyone else, deserve equal access to psychological health mental support and services. Promoting inclusion, understanding, and tailored care can greatly improve their quality of life and overall mental health and well-being.

1.1 Introduction

Mental well-being represents a person's emotional and social well-being. It shows individuals' thinking process, feelings, and behavior, as well as how they handle stress, connect with others, and adapt themselves. Good mental well-being means having a positive outlook on life, being able to handle everyday challenges, maintaining healthy relationships, and feeling a sense of purpose and satisfaction. It is not just the absence of mental disease but the presence of positive mental state. Taking care of one's mental well-being is just as important as physical health and can be maintained through self-care, social support, healthy lifestyle choices, and seeking professional help when desired. Promoting mental well-being involves taking care of both the mind and body through healthy habits, supportive relationships, and seeking help when needed. Overall, mental well-being plays a crucial role in achieving overall health and a high quality of life. Mental well-being is just as important for persons with intellectual disabilities having autism as it is for anyone else. Living with a disability can bring unique challenges, such as social stigma, physical limitations, and emotional stress, which may affect mental health and well-being. However, when PWDs have access to emotional support, inclusive environments, and mental health services and other resources, they can lead happy, fulfilling lives. Promoting their mental well-being means not only addressing stress or anxiety but also encouraging self-worth, independence, and a sense of belonging. A society that supports the mental well-being of PWIDs having autism is one that values dignity, equality, and human potential for all. This study is related to the mental health and well-being of persons with intellectual disabilities and autism. Purposive sampling is used for selecting 60 students with intellectual disabilities having autism from four Vocational Training Centers. The research questionnaire consisted of two parts—a sociodemographic investigation and the Warwick-Edinburgh Mental Well-being Scale used as per the guidelines to measure the PWDs' mental health and well-being. The checklist was explained to the participants for collecting the data. All the participants with intellectual disability having autism had an average level of cognitive functioning indicating a high level of mental well-being among students with intellectual disabilities having autism from Vocational Training Centers in Uttar Pradesh. This may also be very supportive for their academic and vocational skill achievement.

Mental health and well-being is a mental condition that helps people to realize their potential and develop strategies for coping with everyday anxiety and stresses of life, which is helpful in working effectively and actively participating and contributing to society. Moonen et al. (2022) take a look at the necessity of preventing ACEs among students with intellectual disabilities and promoting shielding aspects to reduce the effects on youngsters. Scully et al. (2020) observed that personal functioning was notably related to persons' experiences. Vervoort-Schel et al. (2021) similarly observed a slight association between the quantity of ACE and circle of relative money owed by students with intellectual disabilities and autism. The research spotlights the importance of healthy circle of relative's conditions that protect children from being exposed to detrimental reviews. In instances in which youngsters are exposed to ACEs, Moonen et al. (2022) emphasized the use of trauma-informed care to help youngsters with healing. A study was conducted to perceive the role of computer training in vocational training. This study plays an important role in the well-being of the PWDs as the use of computers makes their life easy, and it is also useful for reading and writing which affects the mental well-being of the PWDs (Bansal et al., 2024).

The study on adults with ASD specializes in normative signs of adult well-being, together with employment activities, but there are several approaches to hypothesize "right" results, and standardizing signs won't be appropriate for people with autism spectrum disorder (Taylor, 2015). For this reason, there have been efforts to conduct studies on autism in adulthood to integrate procedures for assessing individual well-being, in addition to standardized results (Bal, 2018; Kirby, 2016; Lawson, 2020). Moreover, there have been few attempts to systematically have a look at the connection between subjective well-being and professional sports in adults with autism (Goldfarb et al., 2021; McCauley, 2020). Though the literature on normal maturity has recognized a strong association between those two aspects (Schulenberg, 2004) it's uncertain whether a comparable dating exists for persons with autism. There are a few indications that verbally fluent persons with autism may additionally find much less fulfillment from employment activities than normal adults (Black, 2019) and that participation in employment is not strongly associated with the well-being of adults with autism or degree of depression and tension (Hedley et al., 2019). Moreover, it may not be assumed that persons with ID and autism who are not involved in professional sports or engaged closely in volunteers sports have a decreased quality of life than persons with autism and ID involved in extra prescriptive vocational sports for this reason. Another related study described this as a previously unexplored issue. It may challenge existing theories or provide new insights. The proposed research introduces a transformative approach to mental well-being by shifting the focus from symptom reduction to the cultivation of sustainable emotional resilience, cognitive clarity, and social connectedness. Unlike traditional frameworks that often emphasize pathology, this study leverages a strengths-based, holistic model that integrates digital well-being tools, real-time biometric feedback, and culturally adaptive interventions.

1.2 The Purpose of the Study

The study focuses on the major role of mental well-being among vocational training students with intellectual disabilities having autism in a vocational setup. It also concentrates on ensuring that mental well-being can play a major role in successful inclusion. Good mental health is the foundation of a meaningful and fulfilling life. When our minds are well, we feel more confident, connected, and capable of handling life's ups and downs. It helps us focus on our goals, make thoughtful decisions, and build deeper relationships with the people we care about. A person with good mental health can enjoy life's little moments—laughing with friends, feeling proud of their work, or simply finding peace in a quiet morning. On a larger scale, when individuals thrive mentally, families grow stronger and communities become more compassionate and resilient. Good mental health isn't just about feeling "okay"—it's about truly living well.

1.3 Objectives of the Study

This investigation seeks to:

1. Assess the mental well-being of students with intellectual disabilities having autism enrolled in a vocational setup
2. Identify the primary stressors affecting their mental health
3. Explore coping mechanisms and institutional support systems

1.4 Research Questions

1. What are the demographic features of students with intellectual disabilities having autism enrolled in a vocational setup in Uttar Pradesh?
2. What is the level of mental health and well-being of students with intellectual disabilities having autism?

2 Methodology

2.1 Research Design and Context

The research study is an elaborative and correlational project to classify the demographic features of vocational training persons with intellectual disabilities having autism and discover their mental health and well-being. The investigation also measured the differences in the level of mental health and well-being (MHWB) for persons with disabilities involved in vocational training when categorized according to certain demographic features. Vocational Training Centers were selected as the site for this research because there is limited data and little research available in this area that supports and facilitates the work.

2.2 *Sample*

The researcher has selected the sample for this study from different areas of Uttar Pradesh as this is very rare data. The primary challenge for this sample size is the limited population all over India. Obtaining and accessing such samples can be difficult due to their rarity. Purposive sampling was achieved in this study to encourage wider contribution of vocational training persons with intellectual disabilities having autism as clearly explained by the inclusion and exclusion standards. As per disability sensitivity, the researcher has preferred applying the current research to easily available students in the Vocational Training Centers. Selected participants with disabilities were those who met the standards given below:

1. Students with intellectual disabilities having autism enrolled at Vocational Training Centers in Uttar Pradesh.
2. Male students with intellectual disabilities having autism took part as per their availability and convenience.
3. Willing candidates were selected for the research study.

The total number of selected students with intellectual disabilities having autism under the inclusion criteria was 60 PWDs, already enrolled at Vocational Training Centers in Uttar Pradesh. As the sample is rare data. The availability of participants with intellectual disabilities having autism at Vocational Training Centers is minimum in numbers.

3 Procedure

3.1 *Data Collection Tools*

Mental health and well-being were measured with the Warwick-Edinburgh Mental Well-being Scale (WEMWBS), a validated 14-item questionnaire measuring positive mental health. Additional questions explored demographic information, academic stressors, and coping strategies. The questionnaire for well-being of students with intellectual disabilities having autism consists of two fundamentals: a personal background outline and an MHWB investigation. The primary share of the scale assessed the demographic features of vocational training persons who are with intellectual disabilities having autism. The researcher has assembled information for their age group, marital fame, Vocational Training Center wherein they had been registered, and location of house. The Warwick-Edinburgh MWB Scale (WEMWBS) is used for evaluating the mental well-being of persons with intellectual disabilities having autism.

This scale created by a panel of psychologists, who drew on modern literature and conducted different research studies with awareness about students and following psychological analysis. No modifications had been made; for this reason, its reliability was tested. Ethical approval was obtained prior to information series. Participants with intellectual disabilities having autism attended surveys. The information analyzed the use of Excel, using Mean, SD, and Percentile.

4 Presentation of Results

The results are presented in the tables. In total, 60 persons with intellectual disabilities having autism from Vocational Training Centers participated in the study. In Table 1, in terms of the age of the PWDs the majority of persons with disabilities from Vocational Training Centers were between the ages of 26 and 30 years ($n = 60$; 43%), whereas 25% were between the ages of 21 years and 25 years and 32% were between the ages of 16 years and 20 years. Considering the participants' marital status, 37 were unmarried ($n = 60$; 62%) and 23 (38%) were married PWDs. Regarding the academic level of the participants, nearly 65% of the participants were trainable and 35% were educable. Most of the applicants ($n = 60$) had a rural background (30%), urban 33%, and semi-urban 35%.

Table 1 Demographic status of students with intellectual disability having autism from Vocational Training Center ($n = 60$)

		Intellectual disability		Autism		Autism with intellectual disability		Total	
Sociodemographic	Characteristic	$n = 20$	%	$n = 15$	%	$n = 25$	%	$n = 60$	%
Age (years)	16–20	6	30	5	33	8	32	19	32
	21–25	5	25	4	27	6	24	15	25
	26–30	9	45	6	40	11	44	26	43
Marital status	Unmarried	12	60	8	53	17	68	37	62
	Married	8	40	7	47	8	32	23	38
Academic level	Trainable	13	65	9	60	17	68	39	65
	Educable	7	35	6	40	8	32	21	35
Residence	Rural	5	25	7	47	7	28	19	32
	Urban	7	35	3	20	10	40	20	33
	Semi-urban	8	40	5	33	8	32	21	35

n = frequency, % = percentage

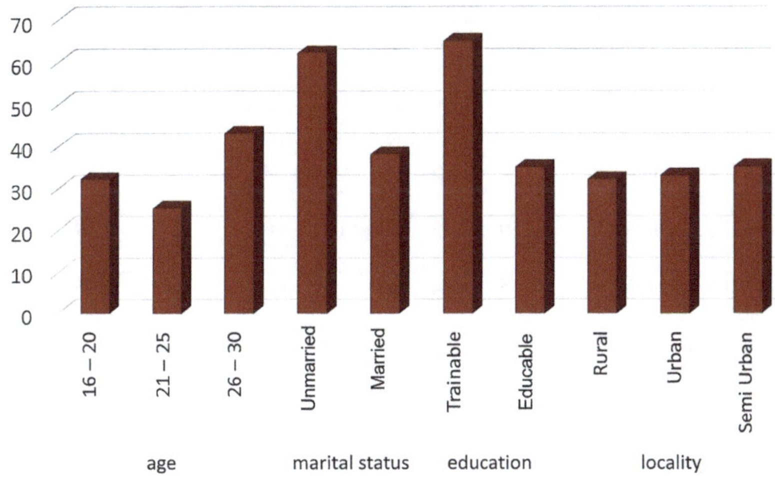

Fig. 1 Demographic profiles of students with intellectual disability having autism from Vocational Training Center ($n = 60$)

As presented in Fig. 1, the majority of the participant PWDs from Vocational Training Centers were from 26 to 30 years ($n = 60$; 43%), whereas 25% were from 21 to 25 years and 32% were from 16 to 20 years. Regarding the marital status of the participant PWDs, 37 were unmarried ($n = 60$;62%) and 23 (38%) were married. Concerning the academic level of the contributors, nearly 65% of the participants were trainable and 35% were educable. Most of the participants ($n = 60$) 30% had a rural background, urban 33%, and semi-urban 35%.

SD = Standard Deviation.

Table 2 shows the mental health and well-being of the PWDs. The maximum score was for item 5 Mean = 03.68, standard deviation (SD) =01.08, which specifies that PWDs often prepare their own minds about their belongings and different circumstances. And different aspects of MHWB indicate above scores in descending order such as 10 Mean = 03.67, SD =01.04, 11 mean = 03.65, SD =01.09, 13 mean = 03.63, SD =01.13, 2 mean = 03.60, SD =01.15, 1 mean = 03.57, SD = 01.13, and 6 mean = 03.60, SD =01.08, respectively. On the other hand, MHWB showing low scores were items 3, 4, 7, 8, 12, and 14, correspondingly (mean < 3.5 points); the lowest scored indicators (item 3) correlated with the contributors sometimes feeling stress-free.

As shown in Table 3 concerning the correlation between and within demographic variables and MHWB among students with intellectual disability having autism, the statistical consequences confirmed that there have been no massive associations among and within the age and their MHWB $F = 0.38$; $p = 0.684$. The marital status of the PWD members and its numerical significance showed that there were least incredible associations within the demographic of the PWDs and their MHWB, $F = 0.61$; $p = 0.437$.

Table 2 Comparison of mental health and well-being among students with intellectual disability having autism from Vocational Training Center ($n = 60$)

Sl.		Intellectual		Autism		Autism with intellectual disability		Overall	
No.	Well-being items	Mean	SD	Mean	SD	Mean	SD	Mean	SD
1	Well-being item number-1	3.50	1.19	4.07	0.96	3.32	1.11	3.57	1.13
2	Well-being item number-2	3.50	1.15	3.67	1.18	3.64	1.19	3.60	1.15
3	Well-being item number-3	3.35	1.14	3.67	1.05	3.64	1.15	3.55	1.11
4	Well-being item number-4	3.45	1.10	3.47	1.19	3.76	1.13	3.58	1.12
5	Well-being item number-5	3.70	1.08	3.73	1.10	3.64	1.11	3.68	1.08
6	Well-being item number-6	3.55	1.10	3.80	0.94	3.52	1.16	3.60	1.08
7	Well-being item number-7	3.50	1.15	3.73	1.03	3.36	1.22	3.50	1.14
8	Well-being item number-8	3.50	1.15	3.27	1.16	3.56	1.16	3.47	1.14
9	Well-being item number-9	3.65	1.04	3.67	1.23	3.56	1.08	3.62	1.09
10	Well-being item number-10	3.75	1.07	3.80	1.01	3.52	1.05	3.67	1.04
11	Well-being item number-11	3.75	1.12	3.33	1.11	3.76	1.05	3.65	1.09
12	Well-being item number-12	3.60	1.14	3.53	1.06	3.40	1.08	3.50	1.08
13	Well-being item number-13	3.75	1.12	3.60	1.12	3.56	1.19	3.63	1.13
14	Well-being item number-14	3.75	1.12	3.27	1.16	3.60	1.12	3.57	1.13
	Overall value of MEAN	3.59	1.12	3.61	1.09	3.56	1.13	3.58	1.11

The numerical effects presented very least correlations between students and their mental health and well-being. Further, thinking about the training and academic level/educational stage of the members, the statistical analysis presented no high correlation between and within the student PWDs and their MHWB $F = 0.03$; $p = 0.874$. In addition to onc's contributors residing in rural, urban, and semi-urban areas, the statistical consequences confirmed that there were no full-size institutions among and in the fitness vocational training students' residence organizations and their MHWB ($F = 0.31$; $p =$ zero.733).

Table 3 Difference between personal background for MHWB (ANOVA)

Variable	Correlation	SS	df	MS	F	Sig.
Age	Between groups	07.59	2	3.80	0.38	0.684
	Within groups	565.39	57	9.92		
	Total	572.98	59			
Marital status	Between groups	5.99	1	5.99	0.61	0.437
	Within groups	566.99	58	9.78		
	Total	572.98	59			
Academic level	Between groups	0.25	1	0.25	0.03	0.874
	Within groups	572.73	58	9.87		
	Total	572.98	59			
Residence	Between groups	6.20	2	3.10	0.31	0.733
	Within groups	566.78	57	9.94		
	Total	572.98	59			

4.1 *Discussion and Conclusion*

This study highlights significant challenges to the mental well-being of students with intellectual disabilities having autism from Vocational Training Center. The findings indicate that the mental well-being of the participants with intellectual disabilities and autism scored highest, which clearly shows that participants were often able to prepare themselves for different situations. On the other hand, MHWB showing low scores reflected the lower level of mental well-being; the lowest score (item 3) correlated with the applicants sometimes feeling stress-free. They have personal, social, and financial stressors that contribute to reduced mental health, while institutional support and strong parental and peer networks serve as protective factors. Targeted interventions are essential to improve mental well-being and vocational training success in this population. Mental well-being is of utmost importance as it directly impacts an individual's overall quality of life. This is the foundation of overall health as this is closely linked to physical health. Good mental health reduces the risk of chronic illnesses and promotes better immune function. It plays a critical role in maintaining energy levels and overall vitality. A stable mental state helps individuals handle stress, cope with life's challenges, and bounce back from adversity. MHWB allows for better emotional regulation, leading to a more balanced and fulfilling life. Positive mental health fosters empathy, communication, and understanding, which are crucial for healthy relationships. It reduces conflicts and supports stronger social connections. Good mental well-being enhances focus, decision-making, and creativity of students with intellectual disabilities having autism from Vocational Training Center. It leads to better performance in academics, work, and personal projects. Lower stress and anxiety level in students with intellectual disability having autism will be helpful in increasing their academic achievement and ability to develop coping mechanisms and institutional support system. Mental well-being is just as important as physical health because it has a severe effect on our thinking process, how we feel, and how we perform our daily activities. It has a great influence on handling anxiety and stress, maintaining relationships, and making right decisions in life. When our mental health is in good condition, we are better able to face challenges, stay positive and motivated, and live with a sense of purpose. It also plays a key role in our physical well-being, as stress and anxiety can impact the body. Prioritizing mental health helps individuals lead happier, healthier lives and builds stronger families, schools, and communities.

Mental well-being plays an important role in every aspect of life, including how PWDs thinking process, feelings, and performance. It has also a severe impact on handling stress, relations with others, right selections, and performance at school, at work, or in relationships. A strong mental well-being helps build resilience, enhances productivity, and improves overall quality of life. Mental well-being refers to a state of mental health where individuals can realize their abilities, survive with normal stress, work effectively, and participate in the community. It involves happiness, psychological, and social-emotional mental well-being and is not just the absence of mental illness. Good mental well-being allows people to feel confident, manage emotions effectively, build meaningful relationships, and enjoy life's experiences. In conclusion, mental well-being is essential for living a balanced and fulfilling life. By understanding its importance and actively nurturing it through healthy habits, social support, and self-care, individuals can lead more resilient, productive, and happy lives. In short, good mental health brings several benefits to PWDs and other individuals and society. It improves focus, decision-making, and productivity, helping people perform better at workplace or in society. Emotionally stable PWD individuals tend to have stronger relationships and improved communication skills. Good mental health also reduces the risk of physical health problems such as heart disease and strengthens the immune system. On a broader scale, it leads to lower healthcare costs and a more positive, supportive community. Good mental health offers many valuable benefits to both individuals and society. It enhances concentration, decision-making, and productivity, which helps people succeed in work, school, and daily life. Emotionally healthy individuals often build stronger relationships and communicate more effectively. Moreover, good mental health supports physical well-being by reducing the risk of illnesses such as heart disease and by strengthening the immune system.

4.2 Implications of the Present Study

The findings of this research study have some new major suggestions for students with intellectual disabilities having autism, PWDs, faculty members, trainers, and administrators at Vocational Training Centers. This is very significant for measuring the MHWB level of student PWDs when admitting them at Vocational Training Centers to find out any possible mental stress and disorder and start to intervene and treat them at early stages, therefore setting up student PWDs for a successful life.

The Vocational Training Center faculty members, principals, administrators, and special educators must work together to draft and revise the policies and guidelines for betterment of PWDs.

4.3 Limitations of the Study

The sample size may be increased to simplify the results of this research. For future studies, drawing from a larger sample size of each disability and from special schools, training centers, participating in a longitudinal layout, and the use of random sampling are key approaches which could provide greater insights into generalizability.

References

Bal, V. H. (2018). Considerations from the 2017 IMFAR preconference on measuring meaningful outcomes from school-age to adulthood. *Autism Research, 11*(11), 1446–1454. https://doi.org/10.1002/aur.2034

Bansal, N., Tandon, M., & Das, H. (2024). Importance of computer in learning of person with disabilities in skill training. *Journal of Applied Research in Higher Education, 16*(3), 966–976. https://doi.org/10.1108/JARHE-05-2023-0187

Black, M. H. (2019). Perspectives of key stakeholders on employment of autistic adults across the United States, Australia, and Sweden. *Autism Research, 12*(11), 1648–1662. https://doi.org/10.1002/aur.2167

Goldfarb, Y., Gal, E., & Golan, O. (2021). Implications of employment changes caused by Covid-19 on mental health and work-related psychological need satisfaction of autistic employees: A mixed-methods longitudinal study. *Journal of Autism and Developmental Disorders, 52*(1), 89–102. https://doi.org/10.1007/s10803-021-04902-3

Hedley, D., Uljarević, M., Bury, S. M., & Dissanayake, C. (2019). Predictors of mental health and well-being in employed adults with autism spectrum disorder at 12-month follow-up. *Autism Research, 12*(3), 482–494. https://doi.org/10.1002/aur.2064

Kirby, A. V. (2016). Longitudinal predictors of outcomes for adults with autism spectrum disorder: Systematic review. *OTJR: Occupation, Participation and Health, 36*(2), 55–64. https://doi.org/10.1177/1539449216650182

Lawson, L. P. (2020). Cross-sectional and longitudinal predictors of quality of life in autistic individuals from adolescence to adulthood: The role of mental health and sleep quality. *Autism, 24*(4), 954–967. https://doi.org/10.1177/1362361320908107

McCauley, J. B. (2020). Defining positive outcomes in more and less cognitively able autistic adults. *Autism Research, 13*(9), 1548–1560. https://doi.org/10.1002/aur.2359

Moonen, X., Festen, D., Bakker-van Gijsel, E., & Vervoort-Schel, J. (2022). A Dutch perspective on two health related issues regarding children and adolescents with intellectual disabilities. *International Journal of Environmental Research and Public Health, 19*(18), 1–8. https://doi.org/10.3390/ijerph191811698

Schulenberg, J. E. (2004). Taking hold of some kind of life: How developmental tasks relate to trajectories of well-being during the transition to adulthood. *Development and Psychopathology, 16*(04), 1119–1140. https://doi.org/10.1017/S0954579404040167

Scully, C., McLaughlin, J., & Fitzgerald, A. (2020). The relationship between adverse childhood experiences, family functioning, and mental health problems among children and adolescents: A systematic review. *Journal of Family Therapy, 42*(2), 291–316. https://doi.org/10.1111/1467-6427.12263

Taylor, J. L. (2015). Longitudinal patterns of employment and postsecondary education for adults with autism and average-range IQ. *Autism, 19*(7), 785–793. https://doi.org/10.1177/1362361315585643

Vervoort-Schel, J., Mercera, G., Wissink, I., Van der Helm, P., Lindauer, R., & Moonen, X. (2021). Prevalence of and relationship between adverse childhood experiences and family context risk factors among children with intellectual disabilities and borderline intellectual functioning. *Research in Developmental Disabilities, 113*, 1–12. https://doi.org/10.1016/j.ridd.2021.103935

Warnick, J. E., Pillay, J., & Munongi, L. (2024). Risk factors related to the mental health issues of selected South African adolescent learners living with mild to moderate intellectual difficulties. *Advances in Mental Health and Intellectual Disabilities, 18*(3), 110–124. Retrieved from https://www.emerald.com/insight/content/doi/10.1108/amhid-02-2024-0009/full/html

Revealing the Unseen Face of Digital Workplaces: How Overload, Anxiety, and Fear of Missing Out Affect Employee Well-being

Reepu

1 Introduction

As the pandemic became a global outbreak, it delivered unanticipated shocks to normal life and the final blow to the old way of working. One especially hard-hit group was knowledge workers, who abruptly became the focal point of what has been dubbed "the world's largest work-from-home experiment." It wasn't just a fix for a crisis but because of that crisis, it quickly became the new normal. Overnight, millions had to move online to carry out their professional duties, which included collaborating with teams, communicating, performing tasks, or learning intellectually. Digital work was no longer elective; it became necessary for business continuity.

And it's interesting that this massive shift to remote work has actually created some surprising benefits. Early data and workplace surveys have indicated that productivity blossomed in a diverse range of industries and professions in remote work. In lots of ways, people said they were accomplishing more in less time with less interruption, and enjoyed the flexibility of working remotely. It means the odds of reversing this trend toward digital work are less likely, not least because of accompanying interest in hybrid or all-remote models, Bunco adds. As they return to work, organizations are rethinking their tactics, and for a lot of them, that means planting their flag in digital workflows.

This change in work patterns hasn't just changed the logistics and operations element but has actually spurred a total rethinking of remote work attitudes. Once upon a time, both employees and management had near paralyzing apprehensions to remote work. Issues of accountability, productivity, and collaboration were frequently the focus of such conversations. Yet the emergence of digital tools as a crisis-driven common good has thrown these assumptions into question. As Park

Reepu (✉)
Department of Management, Chandigarh University, Mohali, Punjab, India

S. Batra (ed.), *Thriving in the Workplace*, Advances in Mental Health and Addiction, https://doi.org/10.1007/978-3-032-06158-4_2

et al. (2021) points out, shared experience of remote work has led to a reduction in the stigma attached to remote working, contributing to a more expansive attitude toward flexible work practices.

Advances in technology have been instrumental in facilitating this transition. The introduction of advanced communication platforms, project management systems, and collaboration tools hasn't only helped on a day-to-day basis, but it has also energized productivity, communication, collaboration, employee engagement, and innovation. Santos et al. (2023) emphasizes that these benefits are relevant to different corporate types, ranging from small startups to big multinational groups. Many companies are finding that these digital tools have also reduced operational inefficiencies and waste, reinforcing the need for digital solutions.

But we must remember that it's not as easy as turning on new technologies to unlock these benefits. Adoption of these tools in the digital workplace demands for a deliberate and intentional combat of these tools' capabilities into organizational activities. Staff will need to be supported and trained to use digital platforms, and organizational cultures will need to change to put outcomes before rigid processes. The extent to which people cannot just survive, but actually thrive, in this environment in which technology is such a pervasive part of their daily work life determines, in no uncertain terms, the performance of the organization.

These personnel are commonly required to remain knowledgeable, participate in and lead teleconference meetings, and perform and contribute to the creation of intellectual output, often in isolation and without physical oversight. According to Cambier et al. (2019), this autonomy of this way of working can contribute to the increase of the sense of autonomy, competence, and relatedness of the employees. Additionally, greater flexibility is a key factor in better work-life balance, which leads to higher employee morale and retention.

But the narrative of digital transformation in the office has a more sinister side. Beyond that, it seems that the infusion of technology into all aspects of work has, for many, come with some unintended adverse side effects. Rather than feeling empowered and connected, some workers say they feel overwhelmed, anxious, and even isolated. The never-ending tide of e-mails, messages, and notifications can cause distraction, digital fatigue, and burnout. This dark side of workplace technology increasingly worries people—and now it's finally being studied more thoroughly by academics.

This literature explores the various ways in which information technology, while beneficial, can also hurt individual well-being, organizational health, and perhaps even generate larger social problems. For instance, excessive use of digital instruments may foster addiction, reduce face-to-face exchanges, and undermine the balance between work and private life. Budnick et al. (2020) stresses that understanding of these adverse effects is on the rise, but the mechanisms by which they function and present are still largely unknown. As companies invest more in their digital infrastructure, it's most important to invest in learning how to manage and mitigate these risks.

In summary, the move to remote and virtual work, which began as a response to the global crisis, has driven a permanent change in how companies do business and workers perceive their professional lives. Though the advantages are clear—productivity gains, added flexibility, and increased innovation—the challenges should not be underestimated. It's not simply a case of embracing technology—we need to approach this multifaceted challenge with a 360-degree frame that extends beyond the technology, considering employee welfare, organizational culture, and long-term sustainability. Only then can the potential of digital work be truly realized and not surrendered yet again.

2 Literature Review

The term "fear of missing out" (FOM) refers to the typical anxiety that people have about the possibility of not having enough satisfying experiences in comparison to their peers or family members. Despite the fact that it also investigated people's engagement in social media, the majority of this research focused on how fear of missing out (FoM) influenced a variety of well-being metrics. According to the findings of this meta-analysis on private FoM, contact on social media may serve as both a precursor to and a consequence of FoM that is experienced. Not only is the consumption of media significant in one's personal life, but it is also significant in many professional domains. One example is that 60% of workers predicted that they would be working from mobile devices in the year 2022 (Roberts & David, 2020).

In order to analyze the fear of missing out (FoM) in professional settings, it is necessary to differentiate between two distinct kinds of techniques that have been used in previous studies. These studies have shown that personal views about FoM might affect the performance of workers in their jobs (Brailovskaia et al., 2023). At work, fear of missing out (FoM) may manifest itself as employees who are concerned about the possibility of losing opportunities related to their position. According to our findings, there is just one prior study that has investigated the phenomenon of fear of missing out (wFoM) in the workplace. According to the findings of their study, the term "word of mouth" (WFoM) refers to the persistent concern that employees may have about the possibility of losing crucial data or career opportunities while they miss work (Zhang, 2023). The first component is concerned with the possibility of lacking fundamental job skills. In contrast, the second component covers the anxiety of missing out on opportunities for networking or failing to maintain key business contacts that other coworkers may have.

When researching fear of missing out (FoM), it is necessary to know that, in this context, contact via social media is just as vital as the use of information and communication technologies (ICT). In spite of this, the link between fear of missing out (FoM) and social media engagement may vary quite a bit depending on the specific topics that are discussed and the theoretical foundations upon which they are based (Fridchay & Reizer, 2022). The majority of research that has been published demonstrates that engagement in social media greatly correlates with fear of missing out (FoM). This association does not necessarily suggest that it is significant for fear of missing out (FOM), which is a small positive correlation between activity in social media and willingness to miss out (wFoM). Despite the fact that there will be 242 million people in Europe using professional social networking sites such as LinkedIn in the year 2023, it is possible that these sites will not have the most significant influence on the day-to-day lives of ordinary workers. The majority of the time, the term "information and communication technologies" (ICTs) is used in place of "social media participation" within the context of the integration of digital technology into the workplace.

Ratheeswari defines the term "information and communication technologies" (ICTs) as any technology that "provides access to information through telecommunication." With the help of information and communication technologies (ICTs), employees are able to maintain contact with their employers outside of regular business hours. Individuals who experience high levels of fear of missing out (wFoM) are more inclined to use ICTs during their leisure time in order to alleviate their feelings of missing out. Earlier research on the universal fear of missing out (Tandon et al., 2021) has shown findings that are comparable to this. Specifically, they asserted that the phenomenon of fear of missing out (FoM) is caused by an unsatisfied want for relatedness or belonging, which individuals attempt to fulfill via the use of social media (Buglass et al., 2017). From a theoretical point of view, the same approach may apply to what is known as the "worst fear of missing out" (wFoM). Individuals who are more aware of the need for relatedness often experience a more significant amount of wFoM and are continually concerned about being excluded by their coworkers. On the other side, expectations related to performance may be the source of wFoM, which is distinct from FoM experiences that individuals have personally experienced. It is not clear from the data that is currently available whether or not such implications apply to the wFoM.

3 Methodology

According to Booth et al. (2016), the identification of qualifying material began with the scanning of relevant databases, followed by the manual search of specific articles and, where necessary, the use of bibliographic searches. Additionally, the use of Google Scholar was helpful in locating gray literature. It was possible to discover additional pertinent research on the subject by using citation searching to identify the articles that were deemed to be the most frequently referenced or relevant via database searches. *Computers in Human Behaviour* was discovered to have the most relevant papers, which resulted in further hand searches being conducted within this journal. The journal had a total of 29 articles. The data collection technique consisted of two measurement sites that were separated by one workweek apart from one another. Participant education on this enquiry was facilitated via digital brochures and handouts.

Hypothesis

Digital workplaces cause stress significantly (H1).

Digital workplace stress directly harms employee well-being, resulting in higher resource losses and poorer mental health (H2).

Stress, in turn, is indicative of a moderating or mediating role in connecting FoM and anxiety with well-being outcomes (H3).

Analysis

Correlation analysis

Stress interacts much more clearly with the other elements, as shown in Table 1. The relationship with higher resource loss is 0.858, indicating that people under significant stress are prone to perceive or feel more physical, emotional, or social resource depletion, whatever their nature. Stress is clearly linked with poor mental health (0.868), FOM (0.886), and anxiety (0.875), therefore underlining its fundamental importance in the interplay of these components. The highly significant associations suggest that in the digital age, stress might operate as both a cause of and a factor aggravating adverse psychiatric disorders.

Worse mental health (0.823), fear of missing out (0.609), and worry (0.810) are correlated with increased resource depletion, which reflects less personal and professional assets. This implies that those who are seriously depleted of resources are more likely to suffer from declining mental health, more intense emotions of exclusion, and higher anxiety. The reciprocal increase between certain psychological states and resource depletion might help to maintain a cycle of vulnerability. These findings highlight how poor mental health could aggravate certain behavioral tendencies and emotional disorders, therefore causing more problems for individuals. FOM, a disorder marked by the dread of being left out of fulfilling events, shows strong correlations with anxiety (0.893) and other variables, including declining mental health (0.928). This suggests that this fear may both be a cause and a result of increased psychological distress because those with higher FOM are more likely to struggle with anxiety and mental health problems. The final variable in the study, anxiety, shows a significant link with all other factors, therefore highlighting its general impact among the related psychological issues. The most important links are with FOM (0.943) and poor mental health (0.932), suggesting that anxiety not only starts from but also aggravates these disorders. Anxiety's significant correlation with stress (0.875) and higher resource loss (0.810) emphasizes its connection with the difficulties and vulnerabilities individuals in modern digital work contexts face.

Table 1 Correlation

Correlations	Stress	Higher resource loss	Poor mental health	FOMO	Anxiety
Digital work place	0.888**	0.823**	0.858**	0.829**	0.844**
Stress	1	0.858**	0.868**	0.886**	0.875**
Higher resource loss	0.858**	1	0.823**	0.809**	0.810**
Poor mental health	0.868**	0.823**	1	0.928**	0.932**
FOMO	0.886**	0.809**	0.928**	1	0.893**
Anxiety	0.875**	0.810**	0.932**	0.893**	1

The study shows a strong correlation: the degree of agreement with stress considerably increases as agreement with the digital workplace increases. For instance, a significant majority (73 out of 81) of those who "strongly agree" with the digital workplace also "strongly agree" that it causes stress. Likewise, the low percentages in the "strongly disagree" and "disagree" categories indicate that a minimal number of respondents reject the digital workplace and its relationship with stress. The two variables show a positive association according to this distribution. Results of the chi-square test support these conclusions. As shown in Table 2, with 16 degrees of freedom, the Pearson chi-square statistic of 283.264 is linked with a p-value of 0.00, therefore indicating strong statistical relevance. The comparatively low p-value of the likelihood ratio test supports this result. These results suggest a statistically significant association between stress levels and opinions of the digital workplace, not some random fluctuation.

The mean square values help to explain this difference even further. As shown in Table 3, with a mean square for the between-group variance of 34.441, much higher than the mean square for the within-group variance of 0.309. This notable mismatch shows how much more clearly the variations in stress levels across groups vary than the group variability. A p-value this low suggests an essentially negligible possibility that random fluctuation produced the differences in stress levels across groups. As such, the digital workplace influences people's stress levels. According to the findings of this ANOVA study, changes in stress levels are connected to opinions of the digital workplace. According to the study, stress levels are much influenced by agreement or dissatisfaction with the digital workplace. This outcome emphasizes the importance of realizing how digital environments affect personal stress

Table 2 Chi-square 1

	Stress					
Digital work place	Strongly disagree	Disagree	Neutral	Agree	Strongly agree	Total
Strongly disagree	0	3	0	0	0	3
Disagree	7	8	0	0	0	15
Neutral	0	0	14	3	0	17
Agree	0	0	0	3	25	28
Strongly agree	0	0	0	8	73	81
Total	7	11	14	14	98	144
Chi-Square tests	Value	Df	P-value			
Pearson chi-square	283.264a	16	0.00			
Likelihood ratio	197.007	16	0.00			

Table 3 ANOVA 1

Digital work place	Sum of squares	Df	Mean square	F	p-value
Between groups	137.764	4	34.441	111.605	0.00
Within groups	42.895	139	0.309		
Total	180.66	143			

Table 4 ANOVA 2

Digital work place	Sum of squares	Df	Mean square	F	p-value
Between groups	157.579	4	39.335	237.254	0.00
Within groups	23.08	139	0.166		
Total	180.66	143			

experiences and the need for particular efforts to reduce stress-inducing factors in digital workplaces. Through better digital work environments, companies may mitigate these challenges, therefore improving employee productivity and well-being.

This study's 180.66 cumulative sum of squares shows the entire range of stress levels across the sample, as reflected in Table 4. There are within-group and between-group elements to this total. Calculated from the within-group sum of squares divided by its degrees of freedom, this mean square is much higher than the within-group mean square of 0.166. This gap in mean square values shows that the variations in stress levels within groups much surpass the random variability within groups. This figure emphasizes the significant differences in stress levels across the groups defined by their perspectives on the digital workplace. A strong F-ratio shows that the variation among group means is statistically significant rather than resulting from random chance. A p-value of 0.00 underlines the statistical relevance of the results. This kind of p-value supports the extremely negligible probability of seeing such an apparent influence related to random chance. The study shows clear proof that the digital workplace influences stress levels.

This analysis estimate suggests that FOM directly influences stress levels, as reflected in Fig. 1. The degree of this relationship emphasizes FOM as a significant psychological trigger for stress, maybe resulting from constant connectivity and the feeling of need to stay updated in digital or social environments. The result also shows a statistically significant association, indicating that more stress definitely causes more anxiety. The small effect size of this estimate suggests that while stress is not the sole element affecting anxiety, it dramatically helps to intensify anxious states, maybe by upsetting mental homeostasis and increasing feelings of vulnerability or uncertainty. A p-value of 0.00 (as shown in Table 5) certifies the statistical relevance of this correlation. This finding suggests that FOM independently aggravates anxiety, therefore confirming the theory that, by prolonging sentiments of inadequacy and dread of exclusion, the fear of missing out causes both acute tension and extended worry.

4 Discussion

Previous studies have continuously confirmed the belief that work telepressure and fear of missing out (FoM) do have a positive impact on individuals' use of ICTs after their official working time. While conceptually different constructs, these

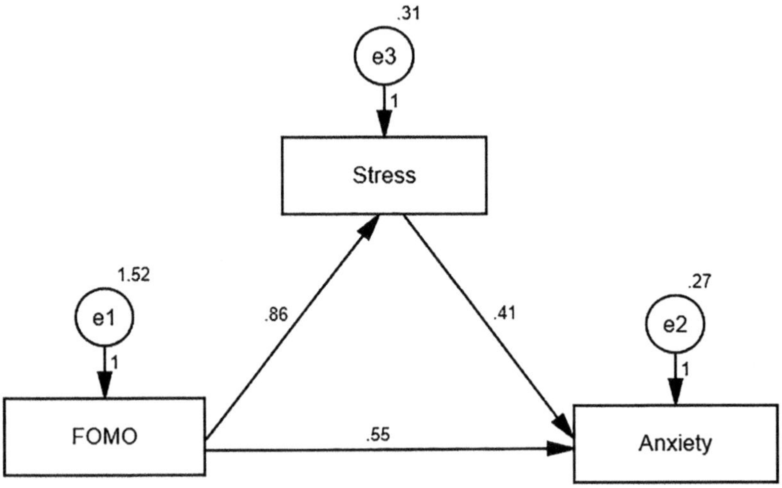

Fig. 1 Mediation analysis

Table 5 Mediation analysis

		Estimate	S.E.	C.R.	P
Stress	FOMO	0.862	0.038	22.879	0.00
Anxiety	Stress	0.41	0.078	5.259	0.00
Anxiety	FOMO	0.555	0.076	7.314	0.00

two phenomena also have some conceptual similarities, in line with theories that explain the continued cognitive effort and behavioral drive to act. Both might be thought of as a symptom of mental aspects driven by contemporary digital workspaces, particularly where the upfront barriers between "work" and "life" are being increasingly eroded by ubiquitous connectivity.

Workplace telepressure is defined in the existing literature as a psychological urge or internal pressure experienced by employees to respond quickly to work-related communications (messages, e-mails, or calls) regardless of the time of day. This compulsion to stay plugged in digitally, it turns out, comes from a combination of perceived pressure as well as organizational norms that can reward, subtly or not so subtly, this type of hyper-availability. Telepressure is closely associated with ICTs since it builds on the role of permanent connection that these instruments enable. Feeling "there is no way to escape" employees who are experiencing telepressure feel they are unable to disconnect, burdened by the perception that they must maintain near-constant vigilance and responsiveness to their communications in order to be considered productive, committed, or dependable.

Meanwhile, fear of missing out (FoM) at work (also known as wFoM) is a central aspect related to workplace anxiety that is "experienced when a person feels that others might be having a rewarding and satisfying experiences to which one was not included". Santuzzi and Barber (2018) refers to FoM as a persistent concern that unplugging from digital professional environments could lead to professional liabilities—e.g., not having an opportunity to influence important decisions or not receiving news that affects work or transparency. Figure 1 shows the role of FoM in social relationships and the digital workplace sharing context: generation and ICT. The traditional field of FoM has been focused on social relationships, yet it has gradually become worthy of consideration in occupational psychology as information exchange is permanently extended to the digital environment.

Owing to the ubiquity of ICTs, both telepressure and FoM are greatly intensified. The easy access and constant communication possibilities presented by Slack, Microsoft Teams, e-mail, and the company's social network can make it challenging for employees to truly detach from work, mentally and physically. Our research indicated that ICTs are not simply passive communication channels but active drivers of work behaviors and perceptions. This is consistent with previous general FoM research where digital media increase fear of exclusion and missing out on communication.

Furthermore, our investigation into workplace FoM (wFoM) unveiled that certain behaviors (e.g., checking messages often, refreshing e-mail compulsively, engaging social media extensively) are not by-products but rather determinants of wFoM and occupational telepressure. Cambier and Vlerick (2022) showed that employees who frequently check the digital channels, in particular outside of official working hours, are more likely to perceive higher FoM and telepressure. These practices are often self-reinforcing: The more one checks messages or scrolls internal corporate communication feeds, the more one gets anxious that something will be missed when not actively monitoring.

This is also a major problem when it comes to workplace stress and mental health. Especially the perceived stress through ICT was positively related to FoM and workplace telepressure. These are considered in the study of Karimikia et al. (2021) to reflect a chronic low-grade psychological stress level, which may accumulate over time and may influence general welfare (Employee digital tethering to their workspace: An examination of the relationship between employees' digital tethers, recovery and well-being by Steven Juras, Konstantinos Korakakis, Sandy J.J. Gould, & Valerie J. Sutherland Abstract). Personnel use of digital tethers may prevent periods of recovery and recuperation, sleep, and time with family or friends, leading to greater levels of emotional exhaustion.

But it needs to be emphasized that in all the studies, also in our study, this does not apply to all findings (significant) according to the tests. Lack of significance for some variables does not necessarily suggest that the relationships are unimportant or are not there, but that they may be conditional on the specific cultural context or be partially due to constraints in the design of the study. For example, though previous cross-sectional investigations found significant associations between message-checking behavior, social media use, and job burnout, our research used a different measure to evaluate several dimensions of burnout. This difference in the approach could have led to different outcomes.

Moreover, the short term of the study period may have hindered the collection of longer term outcomes. Our study was carried out for a duration of 1 week and it might be considered as too short to look at the course of burnout. Burnout, as a psychological entity, usually develops over a long period of time, and is hard to detect during short periods of observation. The Impact of constant ICT use on burnout and fatigue is increasingly being criticized (Andrade & Matias, 2022), asserting that it is less likely to show up quickly, over days as weeks or months of repetitive digital interactions.

For this reason, future work in this area should include studies with longer durations and possibly longitudinal designs, which are able to track the cumulative effects of telepressure at work and FoM. Fatigue as an important outcome variable in further research would help to achieve a holistic view on long-lasting ICT use. This research would have relevance not only to the academy, but also to organizational policy. Understanding the mechanisms through which telepressure and FoM lead to burnout may help companies devise more effective interventions to promote digital well-being.

Interventions might involve clarification about expectations regarding response times and encouragement for digital detox (no worktime or less worktime after work) and boundary-setting behavior, as well as training in time management at work in a virtual context. Leadership can also model good communication strategies (e.g., not sending e-mails after work) which minimizes the cultural influence on telepressure and FoM. In addition, to reduce the stress on employees, a corporate culture that encourages results rather than relentless connections could go a long way.

In summary, ICT use after hours is subject to impact from psychological conditions, such as work-related telepressure and FoM, with potential for increased stress, discomfort, and possibly burnout. These categorizers should not be seen as separate from each other, but are part of a larger culture of digital work that values responsiveness and constant availability. As our results and those of other studies show, the trick is to reconcile the benefits of digital communication—the flexibility and connectivity it provides—with its psychological costs. Hopefully, future research will further the understanding of this relationship—for example by considering longer time-frames and including fatigue-related constructs—and hence also address the question of how digital work impacts long-term employee well-being and organizational performance.

5 Conclusion

It is essential to take into account the developing personal needs given the quick change of the working environment and the subsequent constraints on the workplace resulting from digitalization and remote work possibilities. Using ICT for leisure might help one to control these demands. Still, the body of current studies is not clear on how ICT use fits either a job resource or a work demand. This is significant mainly because the feeling of FoM mediates ICT usage and impacts other aspects of work-related well-being. According to this study, especially with regard to psychological isolation and perceived stress, the impact is primarily negative.

References

Andrade, C., & Matias, M. (2022). Work-related ICT use during off-job time, technology to family conflict and segmentation preference: A study with two generations of employees. *Information, Communication & Society, 25*, 2162.

Brailovskaia, J., Ozimek, P., Rohmann, E., & Bierhoff, H.-W. (2023). Vulnerable narcissism, fear of missing out (FoM) and addictive social media use: A gender comparison from Germany. *Computers in Human Behavior, 144*.

Budnick, C. J., Rogers, A. P., & Barber, L. K. (2020). The fear of missing out at work: Examining costs and benefits to employee health and motivation. *Computers in Human Behavior, 104*, 106161.

Buglass, S. L., Binder, J. F., Betts, L. R., & Underwood, J. D. (2017). Motivators of online vulnerability: The impact of social network site use and FOM. *Computers in Human Behavior, 66*, 248–255.

Cambier, R., Derks, D., & Vlerick, P. (2019). Detachment from work: A diary study on telepressure, smartphone use and empathy. *Psychologica Belgica, 59*, 227–245.

Cambier, R., & Vlerick, P. (2022). When thoughts have no off switch: The cost of telepressure and message-based communication behaviour within boundary-crossing contexts. *Occupational Health Science, 6*, 545–564.

Fridchay, J., & Reizer, A. (2022). Fear of missing out (FOM): Implications for employees and job performance. *The Journal of Psychology, 156*, 257–277.

Karimikia, H., Singh, H., & Joseph, D. (2021). Negative outcomes of ICT use at work: Meta-analytic evidence and the role of job autonomy. *Internet Research, 31*, 159–190.

Park, Y., Day, A., & Barber, L. K. (2021). Time to disentangle the information and communication technology (ICT) constructs: Developing a taxonomy around ICT use for occupational health research. *Occupational Health Science, 5*, 217–245.

Roberts, J. A., & David, M. E. (2020). The social media party: Fear of missing out (FoM), social media intensity, connection, and well-being. *International Journal of Human Computer Interaction, 36*, 386–392.

Santos, A., Roberto, M. S., Camilo, C., & Chambel, M. J. (2023). Information and communication technologies-assisted after-hours work: A systematic literature review and meta-analysis of the relationships with work-family/life management variables. *Frontiers in Psychology, 14*, 1101191.

Santuzzi, A. M., & Barber, L. K. (2018). Workplace telepressure and worker well-being: The intervening role of psychological detachment. *Occupational Health Science, 2*, 337–363.

Tandon, A., Dhir, A., Islam, N., Talwar, S., & Mäntymäki, M. (2021). Psychological and behavioural outcomes of social media-induced fear of missing out at the workplace. *Journal of Business Research, 136*, 186–197.

Zhang, B. (2023). Differential effects of active social media use on general trait and online-specific state-FoM: Moderating effects of passive social media use. *Psychology Research and Behavior Management, 16*, 1391–1402.

Health and Wellness in Modern Workplace: A Bibliometric Perspective on Ostracism and Well-Being

Swati Kadambala, Sireesha Rani Vasa, and Ravi Kumar Karnayina

1 Introduction

Employee health and well-being have become an important aspect in organizations for achieving success in the contemporary workplace (Smith et al., 2021). Studies have shown that integral health and well-being programs improve productivity, enhance job satisfaction, and show low employee turnover (Jones & Taylor, 2018). Nonetheless, despite these programs, workplace ostracism has become one of the leading factors that challenge the feeling of belonging and well-being at workplaces (Brown et al., 2019). Workplace ostracism, as it is known— the experience of being ignored or excluded by coworkers(Ferris et al., 2008)is one that has important consequences for employees' well-being and is related to increased stress, decreased engagement, and adverse mental health outcomes (Williams, 2007a). The negative effects of ostracism affect not only the health of individuals but also the performance of organizations. This chapter examines the relationship between workplace ostracism and employee well-being, with a focus on health and wellness outcomes related to social exclusion in the workplace. The research is based on a bibliometric approach that systematically analyzes the literature to map the intellectual structure of the field, identify key contributors, and uncover emerging trends and themes, thereby forming a critical component of the outlined study (Asmita et al., 2025). Doing so supplies an evidence-based understanding of the way in which ostracism in the workplace affects the diverse dimensions of health and wellness within employees. Learning this will inspire to create healthful workspaces. The results

S. Kadambala (✉) · S. R. Vasa
GITAM Deemed to be University, School of Business (GSB), Visakhapatnam, Andhra Pradesh, India
e-mail: skadamba4@gitam.in; svasa@gitam.in

R. K. Karnayina
Sri Sivani College of Engineering, Srikakulam, Andhra Pradesh, India

S. Batra (ed.), *Thriving in the Workplace*, Advances in Mental Health and Addiction, https://doi.org/10.1007/978-3-032-06158-4_3

gained from the research can offer directions in forming strategies that tackle the impact of ostracism; thus, this can further alter the workplace culture and workforce resilience positively in an organization (Lyu & Zhu, 2019). In an era where organizations are becoming more wellness-focused, the study's findings will be very useful for policymakers, HR professionals, and organizational leaders who are keen on improving the well-being of employees. Tackling workplace ostracism can create more inclusive, supportive, and productive workplaces, which contributes to better overall performance.

The challenges in this modern work environment are multiple: constant upskilling, employer threats of job insecurity through technology, and diversity of workforce. Economic instability, with its associated layoffs and loss of compensation, adds more stress to the employee's life (Akkermans et al., 2020; Callanan et al., 2017; Lee et al., 2018). The COVID-19 pandemic, in specific, has compounded these issues, as emotional and physical well-being are considered imperative, significantly affecting personal and professional lives. Maladjustment on the emotional plane during such moments often leads to increased stress and a feeling of helplessness, hindering career development and life fulfillment (Sultana et al., 2016). In such a situation, workplace ostracism has emerged as one of the major contributors to the deterioration of employee well-being. As a result of ostracism, many unwanted emotional, psychological, and negative physical health issues are produced through stress, anxiety, depression, and burnout, which cause damage to satisfaction regarding jobs, organizational commitment, and productivity (Eisenberger et al., 2003; Williams, 2007b). The World Health Organization underlines that mental health-related problems at workplaces incur additional economic costs, reporting that depression and anxiety alone account for an estimated $1 trillion in lost productivity annualy (World Health Organization, 2022). Beyond the psychological effect, workplace ostracism has been linked to a host of physical health conditions that include chronic fatigue, cardiovascular diseases, and hypertension caused by chronic stress (DeWall et al., 2011; Cohen & Wills, 1985). This means that organizations must design inclusive cultures that support well-being and psychological safety at work. An inclusive work environment is emphasized because employee health and well-being are somehow intertwined with organizational effectiveness. Workplace wellness has evolved from mere physical conditions of the worker and now addresses emotional and psychological elements (Sonnentag, 2018). Under this rubric, ostracism at work emerges as a critical issue because it often has widespread effects on the health of workers as well as consequences for the organization (Ferris et al., 2019). This chapter aims to explore, from a bibliometric perspective, the interaction between workplace ostracism and employee well-being. Mapping trends and identifying key contributors, as well as exploring emerging themes, provides insight into the dynamics of workplace ostracism and how it impacts a healthier, more inclusive work environment.

1.1 Research Questions

For this study and furthering understanding on workplace ostracism and how it impacts employees' well-being, the following research questions will be answered:

- Who are the leading authors in research on workplace ostracism and employee well-being, especially in relation to health and wellness?
- Which journals and countries have made the most significant contributions to research on workplace ostracism and employee wellness?
- What are the main collaboration networks among researchers focusing on workplace ostracism and employee wellness?
- What are the key topics in research on workplace ostracism and employee well-being, and which studies have received the most attention?
- What are the latest research trends regarding workplace ostracism and employee health and wellness?

The importance of workplace ostracism lies in creating organizational strategies for inclusion, improvement in the reduction of social exclusion, and enhancement in employee engagement. Thus, the solution to these will improve employee health, productivity, and performance. Research contributes to the literature of workplace ostracism by giving a comprehensive bibliometric analysis, mapping intellectual structures, identifying trends in research, and suggesting actionable recommendations for future research and practice.

2 Methodology

Bibliometric analysis allows one to know the development, structure, and major trends of a research area by studying patterns of publication, citation networks, and collaboration dynamics (Donthu et al., 2021). For this chapter, bibliometric techniques were used to trace the history of important ideas on workplace ostracism and employee well-being. By citing pattern analysis and keyword co-occurrence, the chapter highlighted influential studies, prominent authors, and emerging trends in the study area. This provided further gaps and regions of study while mapping the intellectual landscape of the field. The interrelation system among articles, keywords, and authors is brought to order; hence, this chapter will present a complete view on the state of literature regarding workplace ostracism and employee well-being, providing, therefore, a clear vision guiding further scholarly investigation (van Eck & Waltman, 2010).

2.1 Data Collection

This research was based on a bibliometric analysis that sought to examine the extent to which workplace ostracism is associated with employee well-being. The primary data in this research were acquired from a huge scholarly database, and Scopus is one of them. This literature search period has been considered from 2000 to 2024, thus crossing over more than two decades. A systematic search strategy was framed that covered relevant keywords exploring the concept of workplace ostracism and employee well-being. The key terms of the research into workplace ostracism included "workplace ostracism," "ostracism," "social exclusion," "employee ostracism," and "workplace ignoring." In conducting research related to incorporating employee well-being, it had incorporated such terms as "employee well-being," "mental health," "resilience," "job satisfaction," and "mindfulness" among other words of phrases, for instance "wellness" and "health," so the research would become wide (Donthu et al., 2021). The initial search yielded 2785 documents, which were then screened through a number of steps to ensure that the selected literature was relevant and of good quality.

2.2 Data Screening

In the Scopus database, a set of filters were used to refine the initial set of documents. These filters included subject areas of Management, Psychology, and Business; document types restricted to peer-reviewed articles and reviews; and publication dates from 2000 to 2024, in the English language. With these filters, the relevant records were narrowed down to 651. The abstract and titles of those papers were then removed with the subsequent screening so that the dataset could have full-text articles only. Therefore, it further made a screening with strong intensity by reducing 215 articles finally fit for the purpose of the analysis of the bibliometric study. These filtering measures ensured the integrity and quality of data while ensuring comprehensive articles were peer-reviewed in light of the research aims and objectives (Bornmann, 2020). Fig. 1 provides a visual representation of document selection process.

2.3 Analytical Tools

VOSviewer, which is one of the highly applied special tools in bibliometric analysis, construction, and visualization of networks, was employed for this exercise as noted by van Eck and Waltman (2010). VOSviewer was used to perform a range of analyses, including co-authorship, co-occurrence, citation, and bibliographic coupling analyses. Such analyses helped in mapping the relationship between

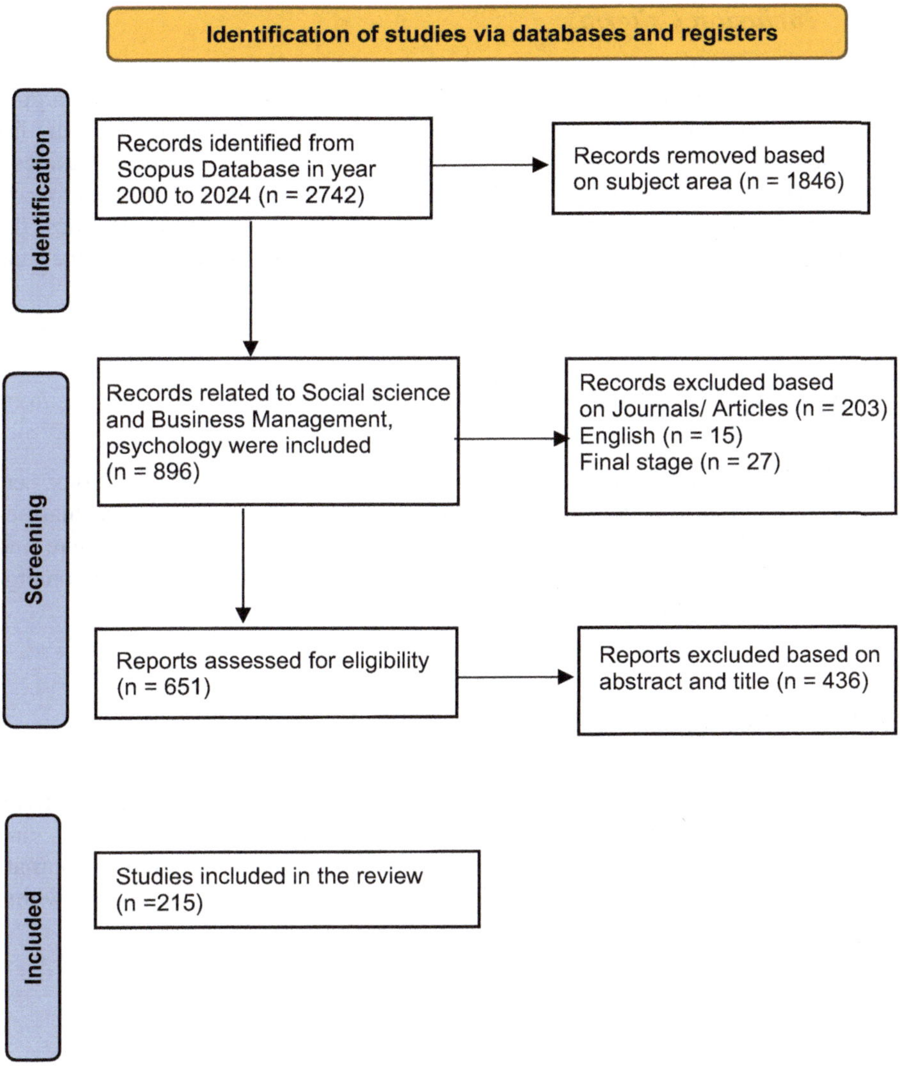

Fig. 1 Source: Authors based on PRISMA 2020 statement

keywords, authors, and citations, allowing for the identification of significant clusters of research, key contributors, and emerging themes within the literature on workplace ostracism and employee well-being. The use of VOSviewer enabled detailed visualization of the citation patterns and co-occurrence of keywords. It thus showed the intellectual structure and evolution of the field, and the methodology helped identify influential studies, the most prominent authors, and the trends in the research landscape.

2.4 *Inclusion Criteria*

In the case of including articles in the bibliometric analysis, stringent criteria governed relevance and impact to select only relevant studies. More precisely, the list consisted only of high-impact journal publications within Social Sciences, Business, and Psychology fields, so the analysis was focused on major contributions toward the understanding of workplace ostracism and employee well-being. Besides, the full-text articles were considered for analysis, not abstracts or titles to deepen the analysis and also its reliability (Bornmann, 2020; Donthu et al., 2021).

3 Results

The results of the bibliometric analysis were organized into three key sections: performance analysis, co-citation analysis, and co-occurrence analysis. These analyses provide insights into the evolution of the research on workplace ostracism and employee well-being, highlighting key contributors, influential studies, and emerging trends in the field.

3.1 *Performance Analysis*

A performance analysis is carried out with regard to research field productivity through the determination of the number of publications, the citation pattern, and the journals. There are 215 articles that have been analyzed from different journals and all were published across 78 journals and mostly in high-impact journals within Business, Psychology, and Social Sciences.

3.1.1 Publication Trends

The number of publications on workplace ostracism and employee well-being has shown a trend that has doubled over the past two decades. The research was less prominent in the early days, but there was a notable surge around 2010, with an exponential increase in the number of studies post-2015 (refer Fig. 2). This phenomenon can be attributed to the rising concern for mental health and social inclusion at work, especially today with the new context of hybrid and remote work environments. Recent studies have emphasized the urgent need to address such challenges to promote employee well-being in workplaces.

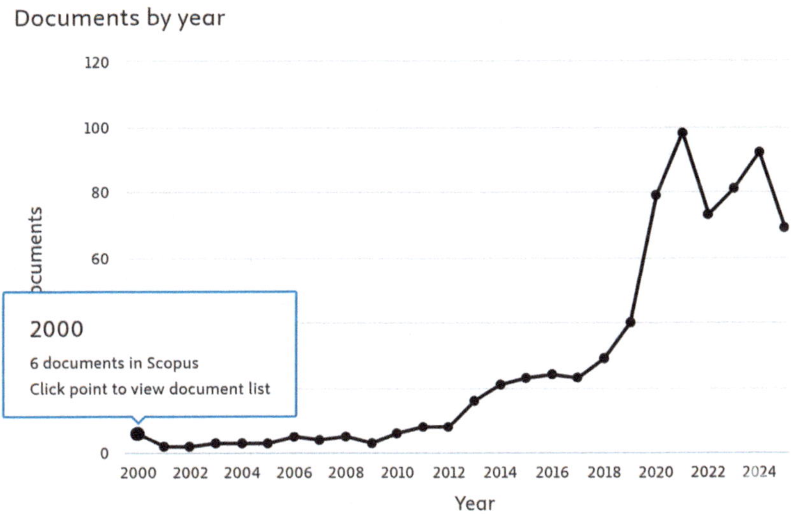

Fig. 2 Publication trend between 2000 and 2024 (Scopus)

Table 1 Performance of authors

Author	Citations	Total link strength
Bingley, Amanda	413	4
Gatrell, Anthony	413	4
Milligan, Christine	413	4
Bentley, T.A.	334	3
Bosua, R.	334	3
Findlay, Robyn A.	334	3
Gloet, M.	334	3
McLeod, L.	334	3
Tan, F.	334	3
Teo, S.T.T.	334	3

3.1.2 Performance of Authors

Most noteworthy contributors include the names of the highest number of contributors with 413 citations and with a link strength of 4, Bingley, Amanda; Gatrell, Anthony; and Milligan, Christine, indicating a network of high interconnectivity or relevance. Secondly, there's also a link strength of 3 and, hence, significantly influential: Bosua, R.; Bentley, T.A.; Teo, S.T.T.—334 citations. Such metrics underscore the establishment and up-and-coming voices in the area of workplace ostracism, providing some rich insight into its development and its key contributors (refer Table 1).

3.1.3 Performance of Journals

The most impactful journals in workplace ostracism research reflect its multidisciplinary nature. As shown in Table 2, *Social Science and Medicine* leads with 9 documents and 582 citations, emphasizing the social and psychological dimensions of ostracism. *Ageing and Society* (451 citations) and *Archives of Gerontology and Geriatrics* (115 citations) focus on exclusion among older employees, while *Frontiers in Psychology* (154 citations) provides insights into psychological processes. Journals like *Stress and Health* (92 citations) and *Community Mental Health Journal* (76 citations) highlight health and well-being impacts, showcasing the broad relevance of workplace ostracism across disciplines.

3.1.4 Performance of Countries

Table 3 presents the performance metrics of the leading countries, where the United Kingdom leads workplace ostracism research with 69 documents and 1734 citations, followed by Australia (29 documents, 1423 citations) and the United States

Table 2 Performance of journals

Source	Documents	Citations
Social Science and Medicine	9	582
Ageing and Society	4	451
Child Indicators Research	3	157
Frontiers in Psychology	8	154
Archives of Gerontology and Geriatrics	4	115
SSM—Population Health	2	103
Journal of Poverty and Social Justice	3	100
Stress and Health	3	92
Community Mental Health Journal	2	76
Autism	2	67

Table 3 Performance of countries

Country	Documents	Citations
United Kingdom	69	1734
Australia	29	1423
United States	49	696
New Zealand	6	427
Italy	7	193
Turkey	4	185
Canada	17	159
Alabama	1	237
Nicholls State University	1	237

(49 documents, 696 citations). Despite fewer publications, New Zealand (6 documents, 427 citations) and Italy (7 documents, 193 citations) demonstrate significant impact. Emerging contributors like Turkey and Canada also add valuable perspectives, while localized research from Alabama and Nicholls State University (237 citations each) highlights high-impact contributions from individual studies.

3.2 *Co-Citation Analysis*

Co-citation analysis was performed to understand the relationship between articles based on shared citations, providing a map of intellectual clusters within the literature. This analysis identified three major research cluster; ,

3.2.1 Co-Citation (Journals)

From the co-citation journals network diagram, influential journals can be identified based on their centrality (placement), node size, and connections. Here's the analysis of key influential journals or references in the field:

Most Influential Journals

As shown in Fig. 3, these journals appear centrally in the network, with strong connections across clusters, indicating broad influence.

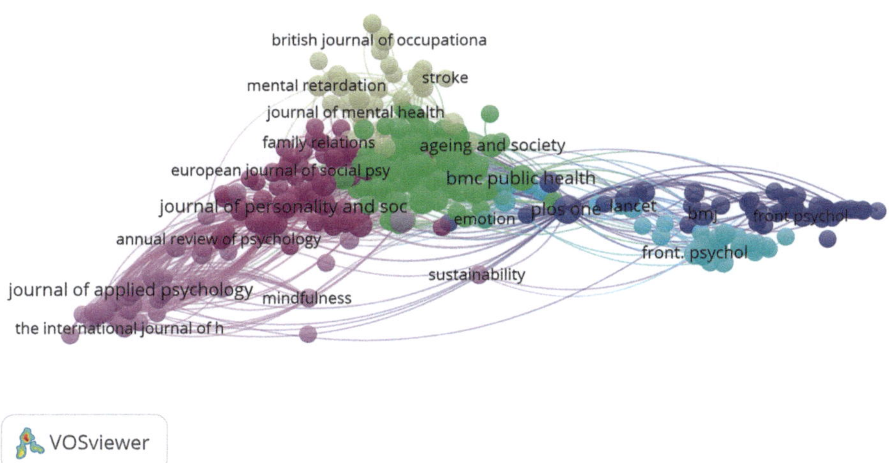

Fig. 3 Co-citation of journal (Source—VOSViewer)

- *Purple Cluster (Psychology and Individual Behaviors)*:
    1. *Journal of Personality and Social Psychology*: Core to psychological research, often cited in studies on personality, behavior, and social dynamics.
    2. *Journal of Applied Psychology*: Focuses on applying psychological principles to workplace, organizational, and real-world contexts.
    3. *Annual Review of Psychology*: Influential for comprehensive reviews of emerging topics in psychology.
- *Green Cluster (Public Health and Social Issues)*:
    1. *BMC Public Health*: Widely cited in public health research, addressing mental health, community well-being, and epidemiology.
    2. *Ageing and Society*: Key journal for research on aging, societal impacts, and health-related issues.
    3. *Journal of Mental Health*: Central in mental health studies and therapeutic interventions.
- *Blue Cluster (Clinical Psychology and Health Sciences)*:
    1. *Frontiers in Psychology*: A multidisciplinary journal at the intersection of psychology and neuroscience.
    2. *BMJ (British Medical Journal)*: Very highly cited in medicine and health research, including mental health and public health topics.
    3. *The Lancet*: A global leader in the health journal category, with a strong presence in the literature of medicine, social science, and psychology as well.

Target journals like *Journal of Personality and Social Psychology*, *BMC Public Health*, and *Frontiers in Psychology* for publications or references in research focusing on workplace ostracism, mental health, and employee well-being. Use interdisciplinary references like *The Lancet* or *Plos One* for broader health or societal impact studies.

3.2.2 Co-Citation (Authors)

Figure 4 illustrates that the co-citation analysis visualizes intellectual clusters within the workplace ostracism literature, with two prominent clusters emerging.

1. *Cluster 1 (Red and Orange nodes):* Focuses on foundational studies exploring social and psychological impacts of workplace ostracism, including influential authors such as Stewart-Brown S., Diener E., and Haslam S.A.
2. *Cluster 2 (Green and Blue nodes):* Highlights contemporary studies on coping mechanisms, employee well-being, and organizational strategies, featuring authors such as Eisenberger N.I., Williams K.D., and Hobfoll S.E.

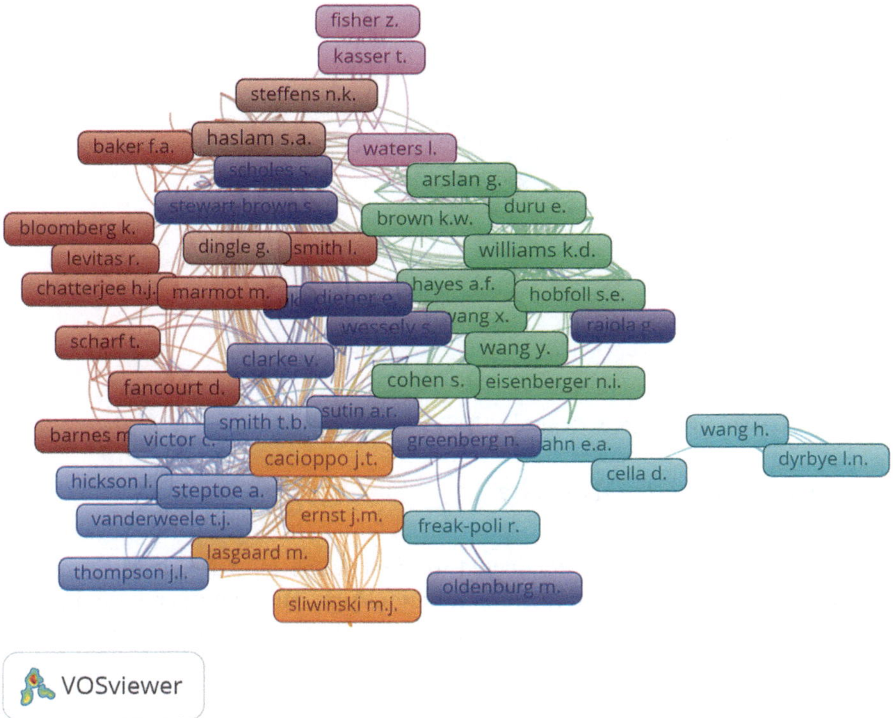

Fig. 4 Co-citation of authors (Source—VOSViewer)

The interconnections between clusters reveal the integration of foundational theories with emerging trends, showcasing the field's multidisciplinary evolution.

3.2.3 Co-Citation (References)

Co-citation analysis was performed using bibliometric data extracted from Scopus database. This technique helps reveal the intellectual foundation of research field by identifying how often two documents are cited together by other works. The resulting network was visualized using Vosviewer, which clustered authors. Figure 5 represents the size of each node that shows the frequency of citations, and the thickness of the connecting lines indicates the strength of co-citation links. Prominent clusters indicate authors such as Braun & Clarke, Cacioppa et al., and Holt-Lunstand et al., reflecting foundational contributions to themes like loneliness, emotional well-being, and thematic analysis in social science research.

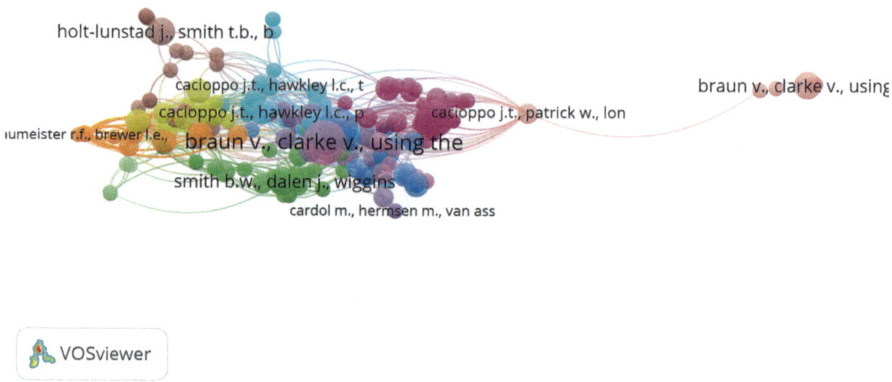

Fig. 5 Co-citation of references (Source—VOSViewer)

3.3 Co-occurrence Analysis

Co-occurrence analysis was conducted to identify the most frequently occurring keywords in the literature and their interrelationships. The analysis revealed several key themes and emerging trends in the research on workplace ostracism and employee well-being.

3.3.1 Keyword Co-occurrence

A keyword co-occurrence analysis was performed to identify dominant research themes. As shown in Fig. 6, six distinct thematic clusters of keywords emerged, each representing a unique focus area in the literature:

- *Pink Cluster (Theoretical Frameworks and Core Concepts):* Highlights psychological theories, motivation, and well-being for an individual. It probably includes basic frameworks or models on the issue of mental health and well-being related to psychological motivations.
- *Red Cluster (Behavioral and Social Interventions):* Represents group dynamics themes and behavioral intervention as well as social psychology issues. Covers interventions and strategies to improve social well-being and minimize social exclusion.
- *Green Cluster (Methodologies and Practical Applications):* Indicates practical tools and applications, especially in measuring and dealing with social and psychological phenomena. This cluster may be on tools such as mindfulness, coping strategies, and interventions for well-being.
- *Blue Cluster (Cognitive and Emotional Aspects):* Appears to have had a great thrust on emotional wellness, loneliness, and social cognition. Outcomes of work or social ostracism have been the centerpiece of psychological or physiological outcomes, mental health, and resiliency.

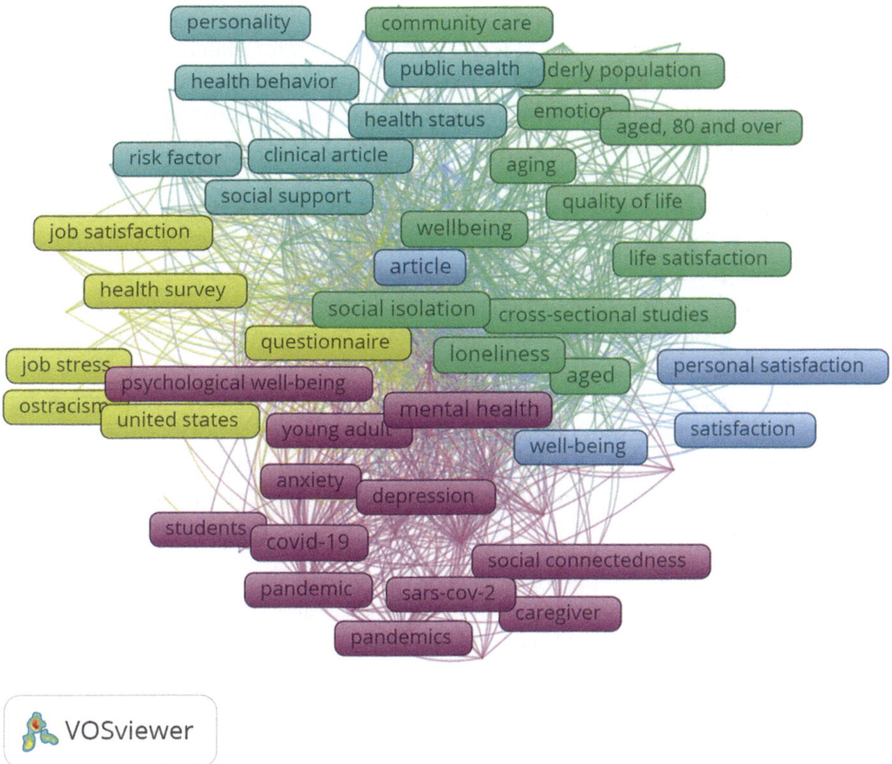

Fig. 6 Keyword co-occurrence (Source—VOSViewer)

- *Cyan Cluster (Healthcare and Clinical Research):* Suggests thematic areas around clinical health, stress management in healthcare professionals, or mental health in healthcare professionals. Addresses the clinical interventions and stress-related disorders.
- *Orange Cluster (Life Satisfaction and More General Outcomes):* Reflects some of the concepts of life satisfaction, quality of life, and long-term health outcomes. It relates to broader societal consequences of well-being and social support.

3.3.2 Key Themes

- *Psychological Well-Being and Mental Health:* The high co-occurrence of the keywords "mental health," "stress," "resilience," "anxiety," and "depression" in the literature indicates the importance of focusing on the psychological and emotional dimensions of workplace ostracism. It reflects the current trend of increasing sensitivity to mental health issues at the workplace, particularly in the scenario of exclusion and social isolation.

- *Workplace Inclusion and Diversity:* The words "inclusion," "diversity," "social support," and "psychological safety" were highly interrelated with ostracism-related terms. This indicates an increasing awareness of the need for inclusive workplaces that foster well-being and prevent exclusion. The connection between ostracism and inclusion is at the heart of current debates on healthier, more supportive workplaces.
- *Employee Engagement and Job Satisfaction:* "Job satisfaction," "engagement," "productivity," and "organizational commitment" were among the most frequent terms highlighted by co-occurrence analysis. This reflects the extensive body of research linking workplace ostracism with adverse effects on employee engagement and job satisfaction, thereby underlining the organizational consequences of exclusionary behaviors.
- *Resilience and Coping Mechanisms:* The words "resilience," "coping mechanisms," and "mental toughness" often co-occur with ostracism-related terms. This indicates that there is growing interest in how employees can cope with the negative effects of exclusion and how resilience can mitigate the impact of ostracism on well-being.

By taking a general perspective, co-occurrence analysis showed several upcoming research trends of resilience, coping strategies, and organizational efforts to better inclusion and diversity in the work environment.

4 Discussions

This chapter provides an in-depth analysis of workplace ostracism and its impacts on employee well-being, revealing several emerging research hotspots, interdisciplinary contributions, and practical implications for organizations. By examining the intersections between psychological, organizational, and health-related aspects, this chapter enriches our understanding of workplace ostracism, especially in hybrid and remote work environments. This highlights some of the most critical future directions in research and practical interventions to mitigate the adverse effects of ostracism on employees.

4.1 Future Research Hotspots

- *Work-Related Ostracism and Coping Through Mindfulness*: Mindfulness-based intervention strategies have captured quite huge attention as an effective platform to counterbalance the negative psychological effects of work-related ostracism. These interventions enhance emotional regulation, resilience, and stress management, thereby enabling individuals to better cope with feelings of exclusion. Mindfulness practice integrated into organizational wellness programs allows companies to equip employees with the appropriate tools for modulating distress caused by ostracism, ultimately leading to an inclusively oriented and mentally resilient workforce. Future studies should focus on the incorporation of mindfulness in workplace settings, especially in relation to exclusion and social isolation.

- *The Role of Hybrid/Remote Work in Mitigating Ostracism:* Hybrid and remote work arrangements have brought new aspects to the way ostracism is manifested at work. Even though some aspects of exclusion, such as physical avoidance, might be alleviated, digital ostracism has become a key issue. Employees working in hybrid or fully remote settings may suffer from exclusion due to non-participation in virtual meetings or social interactions. Further research is required to determine how digital inclusion strategies, such as equitable communication practices and virtual team-building activities, can help reduce digital ostracism. The moderation effects of hybrid work on ostracism and its consequences on employee well-being are important areas for future investigation.
- *Technological Innovation in Measuring Workplace Well-being:* With the advent of AI and machine learning, the assessment and reduction of workplace ostracism become possible. The AI-based analysis of communication patterns can identify the early signs of ostracism, and hence, interventions are made at the right time (Chen et al., 2024). Simulations with virtual reality are also possible, which can help in empathy training and leadership development to encourage inclusive behavior. Future studies can explore whether these technological upgrades are any effective tools in preventing ostracism and improving organizational well-being by also working through privacy and data ethics issues.

4.2 Interdisciplinary Perspectives

Workplace ostracism is a problem that combines psychology, organizational behavior, and health sciences, among others. In the quest to understand and explain this phenomenon, each of these disciplines has contributed valuable knowledge.

- *Psychology:* Psychological research looks into the emotional and cognitive impact of ostracism and reveals its influence on stress, burnout, and mental health (Williams & Nida, 2011). Knowing how ostracism affects the emotions and behavior of employees can thus guide the development of targeted interventions by organizations for affected employees.
- *Organizational Behavior*: There are some research areas that determine the degree to which ostracism is encouraged or inhibited in organizational behavior, such as leadership, work culture, and team dynamics (Eisenberger et al., 2003). Implementing more inclusive diversity initiatives and leadership training would create an environment of less ostracism and build more employee wellness.
- *Health Sciences*: Health Consequences of Ostracism: Mental health-Depression and Anxiety; Detoriation of physical health (Hobfoll, 1989). The solution then

would be integrating the approach involving the treatment both of the impact of ostracism on individuals' physical bodies and psychological states that would be availed through various mental health interventions and wellness initiative.

These dual perspectives indicate that addressing workplace ostracism requires developing an integrated intervention that considers connections at the psychosocial, organizational, and health-based levels to address the causes of ostracism.

4.3 Theoretical Implications

This study enhances theoretical understanding through reliance on explorations of different manifestations of workplace ostracism—hybrid and virtual work. The frameworks have also been expanded in relation to ascertaining how ostracism affects people's well-being and organizational performance in different types of work. Furthermore, regional and cross-cultural variation analysis reduces the much-needed gap left in the present literature so that region-specific interventions can have a better chance.

4.4 Future Research Directions

- *Regional and Cultural Variations*: Future studies should explore how regional and cultural differences influence the experience and response to workplace ostracism. For example, collectivist cultures may exhibit heightened sensitivity to exclusion compared to individualistic cultures (Hofstede, 2021). By understanding how cultural factors shape perceptions of ostracism, researchers can develop regionally sensitive strategies to address exclusion and enhance workplace well-being.
- *Longitudinal studies*: Longitudinal studies are critical for understanding the long-term implications of workplace ostracism on employee health, career trajectories, and organizational loyalty. These studies may help answer how ostracism affects employees in the long term: accumulation of ostracism on mental health, job satisfaction, and career advancement progression (Kwan et al., 2024). Longitudinal studies would further assist in designing intervention strategies tailored to the long-term effects of exclusion.
- *Emerging Role of Technology in Early Detection and Intervention*: Technologies, such as AI and NLP, can track early signs of ostracism through communication pattern analysis. Future research should develop ethical frames of developing these technologies in the workplace so that they are used responsibly and inclusively, as presented by Chen and Raiola (2024). Further, one of the promising areas of future research will be about the effectiveness of AI-driven tools for preventing ostracism and fostering inclusivity in the workplace.

In conclusion, ostracism at the workplace remains a significant concern in terms of employee well-being and organization performance. Addressing new research hotspots through interdisciplinary approaches will help organizations realize more about the adverse effects of ostracism and intervene appropriately. Such emerging research is to be focused on hybrid and remote work environments, technological advancements, and regional considerations toward more effective interventions.

4.5 Limitations

Even though this research is rich with information about the relationship between workplace ostracism and employee well-being, the following limitations apply:

- *Literature Scope:* Only articles published and indexed in Scopus are included. In fact, studies may be hidden in other databases like Web of Science or gray literature that could present additional views which were not reflected in this chapter.
- *Focus on English-Language Studies:* The study only included articles published in English, which may overlook important contributions in other languages. This language limitation may affect the comprehensiveness of the research landscape, particularly for studies from non-English-speaking regions.
- *Cross-sectional Data*: Most of the studies in this analysis were cross-sectional data that only limits one to a lower extent of ability to draw a cause-and-effect relationship between workplace ostracism and employee well-being. A longitudinal study would therefore give better proof of long-term effects.
- *Geographical Bias:* The study was mainly based on research conducted in Western countries, which might have neglected the cultural differences of ostracism experience and its impact on well-being. Further research should examine how workplace ostracism is experienced in diverse cultural contexts, especially in collectivist societies.
- *Technological Integration:* Despite the potential of emerging technologies like AI and virtual reality in this study, technological integration within research on workplace ostracism remains at an introductory level. There is a future need to find out whether such technologies can effectively be applied to real organizational contexts.

5 Conclusion

This study provides a comprehensive bibliometric analysis of workplace ostracism and its impact on employee well-being over two decades of research. Key findings reveal that workplace ostracism adversely affects mental health, job satisfaction, and organizational outcomes while highlighting the potential of mindfulness, hybrid work models, and digital inclusion strategies as mitigating factors.

The research integrates psychological, organizational behavioral, and health sciences perspectives. It highlights not only the theory but also intervention strategies to eliminate workplace ostracism. Emphasis is placed on inclusive leadership, mental health initiatives, and advanced technological tools to create just and supportive environments at work, as suggested by Williams and Nida (2011) and Greenberg (2022). However, to overcome the limitations of this study, future research should extend to non-Western contexts, use longitudinal methodologies, and critically evaluate the use of emerging technologies for intervention. Moreover, research on regional and cultural variations of workplace ostracism can provide solutions that may be applied worldwide (Hofstede, 2021).

In conclusion, this research enhances the theoretical framework of workplace ostracism but also provides actionable insights for organizations aiming to improve employee well-being and organizational effectiveness. Addressing the identified research gaps will further enrich the understanding and management of workplace ostracism in diverse and evolving work settings.

References

Asmita, A., Akhouri, A., Singh, G., & Tabash, M. I. (2025). The silent struggle: a systematic review and bibliometric analysis of workplace ostracism. *International Journal of Organizational Analysis, 33*(3), 502–537.

Berghs, M., & Dyson, S. M. (2022). Affective technologies of social inclusion in disability sports and dance. *Sociology of Health & Illness, 44*(5), 820–837.

Bornmann, L. (2020). *Bibliometric indicators*. SAGE Publications Ltd..

Donthu, N., Kumar, S., Mukherjee, D., Pandey, N., & Lim, W. M. (2021). How to conduct a bibliometric analysis: An overview and guidelines. *Journal of Business Research, 133*, 285–296.

Eisenberger, N. I., Lieberman, M. D., & Williams, K. D. (2003). Does rejection hurt? An fMRI study of social exclusion. *Science, 302*(5643), 290–292.

Ferris, D. L., Brown, D. J., Berry, J. W., & Lian, H. (2008). The development and validation of the Workplace Ostracism Scale. *Journal of Applied Psychology, 93*(6), 1348.

Ferris, D. L., Fatimah, S., Yan, M., Liang, L. H., Lian, H., & Brown, D. J. (2019). Being sensitive to positives has its negatives: An approach/avoidance perspective on reactivity to ostracism. *Organizational Behavior and Human Decision Processes, 152*, 138–149.

Hobfoll, S. E. (1989). Conservation of resources: a new attempt at conceptualizing stress. *American Psychologist, 44*(3), 513.

Smith, P. M., Oudyk, J., Potter, G., & Mustard, C. (2021). Labour market attachment, workplace infection control procedures and mental health: A cross-sectional survey of Canadian non-healthcare workers during the COVID-19 pandemic. *Annals of Work Exposures and Health, 65*(3), 266–276.

Van Eck, N., & Waltman, L. (2010). Software survey: VOSviewer, a computer program for bibliometric mapping. *Scientometrics, 84*(2), 523–538.

Williams, K. D. (2007a). Ostracism. *Annual Review of Psychology, 58*(1), 425–452.

Williams, K. D. (2007b). Ostracism: The kiss of social death. *Social and Personality Psychology Compass, 1*(1), 236–247.

Akkermans, J., Richardson, J., & Kraimer, M. L. (2020). The Covid-19 crisis as a career shock: Implications for careers and vocational behavior. Journal of vocational behavior, 119, 103434.

Brown, S. E., & Battle, J. S. (2020). Ostracizing targets of workplace sexual harassment before and after the# MeToo movement. Equality, Diversity and Inclusion: An International Journal, 39(1), 53-67

Callanan, G. A., Perri, D. F., & Tomkowicz, S. M. (2017). Career management in uncertain times: Challenges and opportunities. The Career Development Quarterly, 65(4), 353-365.

Chen, N. (2024). The impact of workplace ostracism on employee well-being during the COVID-19 pandemic: A study of mediation effects of remote work challenges. Transportation Research Interdisciplinary Perspectives, 26, 101174.

Cohen, S., & Wills, T. A. (1985). Stress, social support, and the buffering hypothesis. Psychological bulletin, 98(2), 310.

DeWall, C. N., & Bushman, B. J. (2011). Social acceptance and rejection: The sweet and the bitter. Current Directions in Psychological Science, 20(4), 256-260.

Greenberg, N. (2022). Mayo Clinic strategies to reduce burnout. 12 actions to create the ideal workplace.

Hofstede, G. (2001). Culture's consequences: Comparing values, behaviors, institutions and organizations across nations. International Educational and Professional.

Jones, R. M., & Burstyn, I. (2018). A conceptual model for take-home workplace exposures. Journal of occupational and environmental hygiene, 15(1), D8-D11.

Lee, C., Huang, G. H., & Ashford, S. J. (2018). Job insecurity and the changing workplace: Recent developments and the future trends in job insecurity research. Annual Review of Organizational Psychology and Organizational Behavior, 5, 335-359.

Lyu, Y., & Zhu, H. (2019). The predictive effects of workplace ostracism on employee attitudes: A job embeddedness perspective. Journal of Business Ethics, 158(4), 1083-1095

Sonnentag, S. (2018). The recovery paradox: Portraying the complex interplay between job stressors, lack of recovery, and poor well-being. Research in Organizational Behavior, 38, 169-185.

Sultana, I., & Sultana, R. (2017). Workplace bullying: a neglected and overlooked phenomenon in the corporate cultures of Bangladesh. International Journal of Management Practice, 10(3), 254-272.

Williams, K. D., & Nida, S. A. (2011). Ostracism: Consequences and coping. Current directions in psychological science, 20(2), 71-75.

Xu, X., Kwan, H. K., Wei, F., & Wang, Y. (2024). Who is likely to be ostracized? The easy target is the Dark Triad. Asia Pacific Journal of Management, 1-28.

World Health Organization. (2022). WHO guidelines on mental health at work. World Health Organization.

Index

S. Batra (ed.), *Thriving in the Workplace*, Advances in Mental Health and Addiction, https://doi.org/10.1007/978-3-032-06158-4

GPSR Compliance

The European Union's (EU) General Product Safety Regulation (GPSR) is a set of rules that requires consumer products to be safe and our obligations to ensure this.

If you have any concerns about our products, you can contact us on ProductSafety@springernature.com

In case Publisher is established outside the EU, the EU authorized representative is:

Springer Nature Customer Service Center GmbH
Europaplatz 3
69115 Heidelberg, Germany

Batch number: 09456952

Printed by Printforce, the Netherlands